I0489963

# CEO Guide to Doing Business in Nigeria

By Ade Asefeso MCIPS MBA

Second Edition

ISBN-13: 978-1499507430
ISBN-10: 1499507437

Publisher: AA Global Sourcing Ltd
Website: http://www.aaglobalsourcing.com

# Table of Contents

# Disclaimer

This publication is designed to provide competent and reliable information regarding the subject matter covered. However, it is sold with the understanding that the author and publisher are not engaged in rendering professional advice. The authors and publishers specifically disclaim any liability that is incurred from the use or application of contents of this book.

If you purchased this book without a cover you should be aware that this book may have been stolen property and reported as "unsold and destroyed" to the publisher. In this case neither the author nor the publisher has received any payment for this "stripped book."

# Dedication

This book is dedicated to Dr and Mrs Ayo Omotoso and their lovely children who seem to have been sent here to teach me something about who I am supposed to be. They have nurtured me, challenged me, and even opposed me.... But at every juncture has taught me!

This book is dedicated to my lovely boys, Thomas, Michael and Karl. Teaching them to manage their finance will give them the lives they deserve. They have taught me more about life, presence, and energy management than anything I have done in my life.

# Chapter 1: Why Nigeria?

Are you a CEO, consultant or entrepreneur interested in entering or expanding your activity in Nigeria?

If you are then this book is for you.

The aim of this book is to give you an overview of the economy and business culture, and potential opportunities. Those new to export will find it a particularly useful starting point.

Nigeria is located in West Africa and shares land borders with Benin in the west, Chad and Cameroon in the east, and Niger in the north. It is the most populous country in Africa and the eighth most populous country in the world. The capital city is Abuja and the three largest and most influential ethnic groups are the Hausa, Ibo and Yoruba.

Nigeria has strong historic, language and constitutional ties with the UK. Globally, it is the UK's 33rd largest export market and the 2nd largest in Africa (after South Africa). The UK's exports of goods to Nigeria were worth £1,235m in 2009 and the export of services was worth £1,311m.

Nigerians often look to British goods and services first before considering any other country, due largely to proximity and the relationship between both countries. British private sector investment in the country is estimated at £1bn.

8

# Chapter 2: Country Profile

Nigeria is the most populous nation in Africa and offers investors abundant natural resources, a low-cost labour pool, and a potentially large domestic market. For many years, Nigeria has had a reputation for being among the most corrupt countries in the world, but the problem has received increasing national and international attention in recent years. Although measures have been taken against both public and private corruption, several business surveys indicate that petty corruption is still widespread and constitutes a major obstacle for companies operating in Nigeria.

The 2011 presidential elections have brought to the surface the large divide between the Christian south and the Muslim north, increasing the political instability.

Positive developments in relation to corruption and investment:

Nigeria has established the Nigeria Extractive Industries Transparency Initiative (NEITI), aimed at improving transparency in payments between extractive industrial companies and government entities, as well as to provide legal instruments to fight for increased transparency in the oil, gas and mining sectors in Nigeria.

The government has set up several investment portals providing oversight and information on investment requirements and business registration procedures (see the section 'Regulatory Environment' under General Information).

Progress has been made regarding public procurement procedures, although corruption persists. Guidelines have clarified procedures, public tenders are now publicly advertised, and observers note that foreign companies are increasingly treated as national companies.

President Goodluck Jonathan signed the Access to Information Law as one of his first acts in office.

# Chapter 3: Strengths of Nigerian Market

The strengths of the market to UK companies are:

English is widely spoken and accepted as the business language.

Same time zone as UK.

£1bn worth of UK investment in Nigeria with leading investors including as Shell, Unilever, Cadbury, Guinness, Standard Chartered, Blue Circle and British Airways resident in the country.

Strong cultural and historic ties between Nigeria and the UK.

GDP growth was around 8% in 2010 and 2011 according to IMF projections.

Lawyers, accountants and consultants well established in Lagos.

Direct flights from the UK to Lagos and Abuja.
Investment incentives in form of Free Trade Zones, and tax holidays.

# Chapter 4: Opportunities in Nigeria

The main export opportunities for UK companies are:

**Oil and gas**

The government has plans to increase oil production.

**Agriculture**

Agricultural potential is largely untapped and the government is keen to attract investment and technical expertise.

**Mining and mineral processing**

The government is considering investment incentives.

**Power (Electricity)**

Scope for private participation

**Communications**

Nigeria is the most lucrative telecoms market in Africa and growing at twice the African average.

## Education and Training

Nigerians are hungry for knowledge and the middle and upper classes prize British standards of education.

**There are also opportunities in:**

Healthcare
Transport
Construction
Aid-funded business

# Chapter 5: Economic Overview

The Nigerian economy is the second largest in sub-Saharan Africa (after South Africa), with a total GDP in 2009 of US$168.8 billion. Large reserves of natural resources mean Nigeria has the potential to build a highly prosperous economy, but decades of economic mismanagement and widespread corruption have placed Nigeria amongst the poorest 20 nations in the world. However, this situation is changing following the introduction of democratic rule in 1999.

The current government has identified corruption and governance as issues that need to be forcefully tackled and an Anti-Corruption Bill was recently been signed into law.

Most economic activity occurs in 4 main cities: Lagos, Kaduna, Port Harcourt, and Abuja. The economy is dominated by oil and gas, which accounts for approximately 40% of GDP, followed by agriculture about 33% of GDP.

Recent high oil prices have boosted revenue leaving the public finances in relatively good shape. However increased public spending has stoked inflationary pressures.

The IMF projects Nigeria's GDP growth in 2010 to be 7.3%. Oil-rich Nigeria, long hobbled by political instability, corruption, inadequate infrastructure, and poor macroeconomic management, has undertaken several reforms over the past decade.

Nigeria's former military rulers failed to diversify the economy away from its overdependence on the capital-intensive oil sector, which provides 95% of foreign exchange earnings and about 80% of budgetary revenues. Following the signing of an IMF stand-by agreement in August 2000, Nigeria received a debt-restructuring deal from the Paris Club and a $1 billion credit from the IMF, both contingents on economic reforms.

Nigeria pulled out of its IMF program in April 2002, after failing to meet spending and exchange rate targets, making it ineligible for additional debt forgiveness from the Paris Club.

Since 2008 the government has begun showing the political will to implement the market-oriented reforms urged by the IMF, such as to modernize the banking system, to curb inflation by blocking excessive wage demands, and to resolve regional disputes over the distribution of earnings from the oil industry.

In 2003, the government began deregulating fuel prices, announced the privatization of the country's four oil refineries, and instituted the National Economic Empowerment Development Strategy, a domestically designed and run program modeled on the IMF's Poverty Reduction and Growth Facility for fiscal and monetary management.

In November 2005, Abuja won Paris Club approval for a debt-relief deal that eliminated $18 billion of debt in exchange for $12 billion in payments - a total package worth $30 billion of Nigeria's total $37 billion external debt. The deal requires Nigeria to be subject to stringent IMF reviews. Based largely on increased oil exports and high global crude prices, GDP rose strongly in 2007 and 2008.

President YAR'ADUA and Goodluck Jonathan pledged to continue the economic reforms of their predecessor with emphasis on infrastructure improvements. Infrastructure is the main impediment to growth. The government is working toward developing stronger public-private partnerships for electricity and roads.

## GDP (purchasing power parity)

$336.2 billion (2008 est.)
Country comparison to the world: 36
$319.3 billion (2007 est.)
$300.1 billion (2006 est.)
Note: data are in 2008 US dollars

## GDP (official exchange rate)

$207.1 billion (2008 est.)

## GDP - real growth rate

5.3% (2008 est.)
Country comparison to the world: 82
6.4% (2007 est.)
6.2% (2006 est.)

## GDP - per capita (PPP)

$2,300 (2008 est.)
Country comparison to the world: 182
$2,200 (2007 est.)
$2,100 (2006 est.)
Note: data are in 2008 US dollars

## GDP - composition by sector

Agriculture: 18.1%
Industry: 50.8%
Services: 31.1% (2008 est.)

## Labour force

51.04 million (2008 est.)
Country comparison to the world: 10
Labour force - by occupation:

Agriculture: 70%
Industry: 10%
Services: 20% (1999 est.)

## Unemployment rate

4.9% (2007 est.)
Country comparison to the world: 61

## Population below poverty line

70% (2007 est.)

## Household income or consumption by percentage share

Lowest 10%: 2%
Highest 10%: 32.4% (2004)

## Distribution of family income - Gini index

43.7 (2003)
Country comparison to the world: 48
50.6 (1997)

## Investment (gross fixed)

21.7% of GDP (2008 est.)
Country comparison to the world: 88

## Public debt

13.4% of GDP (2008 est.)
Country comparison to the world: 110
20% of GDP (2004 est.)

## Inflation rate (consumer prices)

11.6% (2008 est.)
Country comparison to the world: 167
5.4% (2007 est.)

## Central bank discount rate

9.75% (31 December 2008)
Country comparison to the world: 46
9.5% (31 December 2007)

## Commercial bank prime lending rate

15.48% (31 December 2008)
Country comparison to the world: 31
16.94% (31 December 2007)

## Stock of money

$35.29 billion (31 December 2008)
Country comparison to the world: 25
$26.82 billion (31 December 2007)

## Stock of quasi money

$32.04 billion (31 December 2008)
Country comparison to the world: 36
$22.78 billion (31 December 2007)

## Stock of domestic credit

$49.51 billion (31 December 2008)
Country comparison to the world: 49
$35.68 billion (31 December 2007)

## Market value of publicly traded shares

$49.8 billion (31 December 2008)
Country comparison to the world: 51
$86.35 billion (31 December 2007)
$32.82 billion (31 December 2006)

## Agriculture - products

cocoa, peanuts, palm oil, corn, rice, sorghum, millet, cassava (tapioca), yams, rubber; cattle, sheep, goats, pigs; timber; fish

## Industries

crude oil, coal, tin, columbite; palm oil, peanuts, cotton, rubber, wood; hides and skins, textiles, cement and other construction materials, food products, footwear, chemicals, fertilizer, printing, ceramics, steel, small commercial ship construction and repair

## Industrial production growth rate

2.8% (2008 est.)
Country comparison to the world: 88

## Electricity - production

21.92 billion kWh (2007 est.)
Country comparison to the world: 69

## Electricity - consumption

19.21 billion kWh (2007 est.)
Country comparison to the world: 68

## Electricity - exports

0 kWh (2008 est.)

**Electricity - imports**

0 kWh (2008 est.)

**Oil - production**

2.169 million bbl/day (2008 est.)
Country comparison to the world: 16

**Oil - consumption**

286,000 bbl/day (2008 est.)
Country comparison to the world: 45

**Oil - exports**

2.327 million bbl/day (2007 est.)
Country comparison to the world: 8

**Oil - imports**

170,000 bbl/day (2007 est.)
Country comparison to the world: 54

**Oil - proved reserves**

36.22 billion bbl (1 January 2009 est.)
Country comparison to the world: 10

**Natural gas - production**

32.82 billion cu m (2008 est.)
Country comparison to the world: 25

## Natural gas - consumption

12.28 billion cu m (2008 est.)
Country comparison to the world: 46

## Natural gas - exports

20.55 billion cu m (2008)
Country comparison to the world: 11

## Natural gas - imports

0 cu m (2008 est.)
Country comparison to the world: 147

## Natural gas - proved reserves

5.215 trillion cu m (1 January 2009 est.)
Country comparison to the world: 7

## Current account balance

$3.877 billion (2008 est.)
Country comparison to the world: 37
$2.203 billion (2007 est.)

## Exports

$76.03 billion (2008 est.)
Country comparison to the world: 43
$61.82 billion (2007 est.)

**Exports - commodities**

Petroleum and petroleum products 95%, cocoa, rubber

**Exports - partners**

US 41.4%, India 10.4%, Brazil 9.4%, Spain 7.2%, France 4.6% (2008)

**Imports**

$46.3 billion (2008 est.)
Country comparison to the world: 52
$38.8 billion (2007 est.)

**Imports - commodities**

Machinery, chemicals, transport equipment, manufactured goods, food and live animals

**Imports - partners**

China 13.8%, Netherlands 9.6%, US 8.4%, UK 5.3%, South Korea 5.2%, France 4.3% (2008)

**Reserves of foreign exchange and gold**

$53 billion (31 December 2008 est.)
Country comparison to the world: 23
$51.33 billion (31 December 2007 est.)

## Stock of direct foreign investment - at home

$68.84 billion (31 December 2008 est.)
Country comparison to the world: 44
$58.84 billion (31 December 2007 est.)

## Stock of direct foreign investment - abroad

$13.02 billion (31 December 2008 est.)
Country comparison to the world: 43
$12.72 billion (31 December 2007 est.)

## Population

Nigeria has a population of over 150 million people spread across the 36 states, with considerably higher population concentrations in the urban areas.

Hausa, Yoruba and Ibo are the largest ethnic groups, but there are also over 250 other minor groups, some numbering fewer than 10,000 people. The other large groups are Edo, Fulani, Gwari, Ibibio, Idoma, Igala, Ijaw, Junkun, Kanuri, Nupe, Tiv and Urhobo.

# Chapter 6: Political Overview

Nigeria is a federal republic modelled on the United States, with executive power exercised by the president and legislative powers shared by a bicameral legislature, with the upper and lower Houses of Assembly, like the Senate and the House of Representatives.

The president is both Head of State and Head of Government and elected by popular vote to a maximum of two four-year terms. The current president is Goodluck Jonathan who was previously Vice President to former President Umaru Musa Yar'Adua. President Yar'Adua died in 2010 after spending three years in office following his election in 2007.

Tribal, ethnic and religious biases have played a visible role in Nigerian politics both before and since independence in 1960. Corruption persists among public office holders despite the establishment of anti-corruption bodies like the Economic and Financial Crimes Commission (EFCC).

The Niger-Delta region, which is Nigeria's oil-producing region, has in the last five years witnessed a number of militant attacks and kidnappings.

Demonstrations and outbreaks of localised civil unrest and violence can occur with little notice throughout the country. The security situation may deteriorate rapidly in the vicinity of political gatherings. If you encounter a threatening or intimidating situation do not try to make your way through it. Turn round and go home.

Before planning any official or recreational travel, particularly by road, you should check whether any political rallies or demonstrations are planned for a particular area, or on your route.

# Chapter 7: Getting There

## Visas

All British nationals must hold a valid visa to enter Nigeria. British nationals planning to work in Nigeria must obtain the correct visa before doing so. For further information on entry requirements, please contact the Nigerian High Commission in London.

## By Air

There are a number of private airlines, including charters, serving cities throughout Nigeria. Domestic flights link Lagos with Abuja, Benin City, Calabar, Enugu, Jos, Kaduna, Kano, Maiduguri, Port Harcourt, Sokoto, Warri and Yola.

Domestic airport information can be found on the FAAN website.

Murtala Mohammed Airport in Ikeja, Lagos, is Nigeria's main international airport. It is 16 miles from the city centre and is served by most major European airlines including BA, Virgin Atlantic, KLM, Air France and Lufthansa. Nigerian Arik Air began flying from Lagos to Heathrow in 2005.

The other international airports are in Abuja, Kano and Port Harcourt. It is recommended that visitors are met at the airport

## Car Hire

Car hire is available from international hotels and Avis and Hertz also have offices in Lagos.

Car hire usually includes a local driver and insurance cover. Always negotiate the price in advance.

# Chapter 8: Local Travel

Nigeria experiences heavy rainfall during the wet season (June - September) and flash flooding can occur. Water-borne disease poses a greater risk during the rainy season; there have been reports of cholera in Oyo State recently due to flooding.

Northern Nigeria

If you are travelling in northern Nigeria you should take extra precautions and avoid crowds. Violence could erupt quickly and without warning.

There has been an increase in terrorism in northern Nigeria since Boko Haram publicly declared its support for Al Qaeda in 2010. The group has been responsible for a number of terrorist attacks in the north.

A curfew from 23:00 - 06:00 in Kaduna City remains in place.

I advise against all travel to:

Borno State

I advise against all but essential travel to:

Plateau State (including Jos)
The Niger Delta States

I advise against all travel to:

The Niger Delta States of Delta, Bayelsa and Rivers (including Port Harcourt) and to the riverine areas of Akwa Ibom State (i.e. the river and swamp locations on or close to the coast accessible by boat, but not by road). The foreign office recently advise British nationals in these areas to leave.

I advise against all but essential travel to:

All other areas of Akwa Ibom State; I also advise against all travel to the area bordering Cameroon in the region of the Bakassi Peninsula, where local feelings remain sensitive after the resolution of a border dispute in 2008.

You should avoid going to public places in Port Harcourt frequented by expatriates, including bars and restaurants. If you encounter a threatening or intimidating situation do not try to make your way through it; turn around and go home. I have received reports of an attempt to try to lure an expatriate to a meeting at a remote location near Port Harcourt. It is believed that this was an attempted kidnap.

When arranging meetings in Nigeria you should ensure that the contact is known to you, and that the meeting is held at a secure location.

The High Commission Liaison Office and British Council in Port Harcourt are subject to closure at short notice. Closure and reopening of the offices will be reflected in this travel advice.

If you decide to travel to or remain in these areas it would be reckless to do so unless and until you have taken full, appropriate professional security advice and have acted on it.

Many companies have introduced strict restrictions on travel. If you are a resident British national, you should follow your employer's local security guidelines. In addition:

You must be vigilant at all times and make sure that your local host and family know your travel plans and timings.

You should register with the British Deputy High Commission in Lagos on arrival.

Limit your movements to only essential journeys.

Vary your routines.

If travelling by road you should only travel in fully protected transport and aim to complete your journey well before nightfall.

Keep your car doors locked and windows closed and maintain telephone or radio communications to report your movements.

You should consider permanent armed protection, but be aware that even this cannot guarantee your safety.

# Chapter 9: Road Travel

Traffic travels on the right. There is an extensive road network throughout Nigeria, with tarmac roads, some severely pot-holed, linking the major cities. In some areas secondary roads are liable to become impassable for periods during the rains. The major cities suffer from severe congestion, and long hold-ups can occur. Use of local taxis or buses is not recommended.

Traffic in many of Nigeria's major cities can be chaotic and slow moving. Serious traffic jams in Lagos are not uncommon. Short journeys that normally take minutes can sometimes take hours. I advise you to take a mobile telephone with you when travelling by car so that you can stay in touch with family, friends and employers. We also advise you to have a supply of bottled water in your vehicle at all times.

There are authorised as well as unauthorised vehicle checkpoints throughout Nigeria. Some are for security checks, others to extort small payments of money. You should slow down at any type of checkpoint and use common sense at all times.

There are frequent reports of robberies and car-jackings, some involving armed gunmen, on Nigeria's urban and rural road network. If you are involved in a car-jacking, experience has shown that victims who comply immediately and fully with the attackers' demands are left unharmed.

**You should:**

- Be vigilant when travelling on all major roads within Nigeria.
- Avoid any travel after dark outside city centres.
- Take care after dark within cities, avoiding secondary roads and areas where other traffic is light.
- Be particularly vigilant when sitting in traffic jams or at traffic lights at night, and where street lighting is poor.
- Keep your car windows and doors locked and valuables out of sight.
- If you feel your vehicle is being followed, you should drive to the nearest place of safety - e.g. to the nearest police station.

Public transport is dangerous. Taxis and long distance buses are poorly maintained and are often uninsured and driven by fraudulent drivers.

Most major hotels offer cars for hire with drivers. We would recommend that you use these where possible.

If you are expecting a greeter or driver to collect you at any of Nigeria's international airports you should ensure that he/she can properly identify themselves, as bogus greeters are a problem.

On 28 June 2011 the Ministry of the Federal Capital Territory put in place new security measures in Abuja, including parking restrictions in the Central Business District, a closing time of 2200 for recreational facilities (cinemas, clubs and bars) and 1800 for parks and gardens that admit children.

Road travel in Abuja and Lagos is banned between 07:00 and 10:00 on the last Saturday of every month for municipal road clean up; police vigilantly enforce the ban.

# Chapter 10: Air, Sea and Railway Travel

## Air

The EU has published a list of air carriers that are subject to an operating ban or restrictions within the EU.

Airlines flying between Nigeria and London can occasionally become severely overbooked. As a result, airlines advise travellers to reconfirm their return booking at least 48 hours before they are due to depart, and to check in early.

Following a series of crashes, there are also concerns about the safety and reliability of some airline companies operating domestic flights within Nigeria.

## Sea

There have been attacks of piracy/armed robbery against ships at anchor in Nigerian waters and at many of the rivers and harbours in the Niger Delta area. I advise mariners to take appropriate precautions.

## Railways

There are approximately 3,500 kilometres of railway in Nigeria. There are nominally two main rail lines between Lagos and Kano and between Port Harcourt and Kano. However, lack of investment and maintenance (and the use of tracks for makeshift building works) has left the network fragmented and largely unusable.

There are also branch lines to Kaura Namoda, Nguru, Baro, Jos and Maiduguri

# Chapter 11: Requirements to Live and Work in Nigeria

Combined Expatriate Residence Permit and Aliens Card (CERPAC) 'Aliens Card'

The 'Aliens Card' is the Residence Permit for expatriates (except ECOWAS citizens), accredited diplomats and children below the age of 16 years. All British nationals resident in Nigeria are required to apply for the card, except children below the age of 15, who live with their parents, unless the parents specifically request the card. Any British National staying in Nigeria for more than 56 days must obtain an Aliens Card.

British nationals relocating to a different part of Nigeria must inform the nearest Aliens Office.

When a British national holding an Aliens Card leaves Nigeria permanently, the card must be handed in to the Aliens Office.

All British nationals travelling to Nigeria must hold a valid visa before entering the country. British nationals planning to work in Nigeria must obtain the correct visa before doing so. For further information on entry requirements, I advise visitors to contact the Nigeria High Commission in London.

**Passport validity**

You must hold a valid passport to enter Nigeria. Your passport must be valid for a minimum period of six months from the date of entry into Nigeria.

**Travelling with children**

Single parents or other adults travelling alone with children should be aware that some countries require documentary evidence of parental responsibility before allowing lone parents to enter the country or, in some cases, before permitting the children to leave the country. For further information on exactly what will be required at immigration please contact the Nigeria High Commission in London.

**Health**

Basic, limited medical facilities are available in some parts of Nigeria.

You should seek medical advice before travelling to Nigeria and ensure that all appropriate vaccinations are up to date. For further information on vaccination requirements, health outbreaks and general disease protection and prevention you should visit the websites of the National Travel Health Network and Centre (NaTHNaC) and NHS Scotland's Fit For Travel.

Malaria is very common in Nigeria and prophylaxis is recommended in all areas of the country. Travellers should also protect themselves from insect bites. It is estimated that 25% of all malaria cases in the world happen in Nigeria. It is therefore essential for all travellers to take appropriate precautions.

Cholera, measles, meningitis and other communicable diseases do occur in Nigeria and most years there is an outbreak.

It is recommended that travel health information services are consulted before travel. Nigeria is also one of last countries in the world with wild circulating polio virus. This can be prevented through immunisation prior to arrival.

Most ill health can be prevented by following good hygiene practices and following advice of health professionals.

It is estimated that 3.1 million Nigerians are living with HIV; the prevalence rate is estimated at around 3.6% of the adult population. This compares to the prevalence rate in adults in the UK of around 0.2%. You should exercise normal precautions to avoid exposure to HIV/AIDS.

# Chapter 12: Local Laws and Customs

Nigeria has the largest Muslim population in sub-Saharan Africa. You should exercise discretion in behaviour and dress, particularly in the north and during the Holy month of Ramadan and when visiting religious sites.

The Sharia penal code has been introduced in 12 northern states (Sokoto, Zamfara, Kebbi, Kano, Yobe, Borno, Katsina, Jigawa, Bauchi, Kaduna, Niger and Gombe). Homosexuality by Muslims in those states can attract a sentence of 100 lashes if the defendant is unmarried or stoning if married or divorced.

Alcohol consumption, infidelity and theft can attract harsh sentences including stoning, amputation, lashings or long prison terms. Non-Muslims are not bound by Sharia law.

Homosexuality is illegal under Federal law, covering the whole of Nigeria.

Possession, use of or trafficking in illegal drugs is a serious offence and can result in lengthy prison sentences and heavy fines.

It is illegal to import beer, mineral water, soft drinks, sparkling wine, fruits, vegetables, cereals, eggs, textile fabrics, jewellery, and precious metals. It is illegal to export pieces of African art, particularly antiques, without written authorisation from the Department of Antiquities. You should contact the Nigeria High Commission in London for specific information regarding customs requirements.

Photography in airports may lead to arrest.

# Chapter 13: Preparing to Export to Nigeria

AA Global Sourcing Ltd (http://www.aaglobalsourcing.com) assists UK companies preparing to export to Nigeria. It can conduct market research, identify distributors and agents, provide validated lists of potential customers, organise visit programmes and promotional events.

We can help you commission UKTI's Overseas Market Introduction Services (OMIS) to assist your company to enter or expand your business in Nigeria. Under this service UKTI staff at the High Commission, who have wide local experience and knowledge; can provide the support and advice most relevant to your company's specific needs in the market.

**Local representation**

Nigeria is a highly competitive market, so good local representation is vital to determine the way in which a particular good or service is marketed in the country.

Before establishing formal agreements, it is important that exporters understand the sales strategy of their potential representative. It is normal, but not obligatory to give sole representative rights for the whole country to one agent. This may initially be agreed for one year with a performance-tied option to extend for a longer period.

It is advised that exporters visit Nigeria regularly. Such visits are invaluable to the exporter to understand local market conditions.

It is strongly recommended that companies seek legal advice when drawing up contracts with agents. AA Global Sourcing Ltd (http://www.aaglobalsourcing.com) can supply a list of lawyers.

**Labelling and Packaging regulations**

Shippers must ensure that Import Duty Report (IDR) numbers are always quoted on the shipping manifests for all shipments into the country before such manifests are submitted to the Nigeria Customs Service.

For air cargo, the airline must ensure that the IDR number for the goods being carried is stated on the airway bill.

A Certificate of Analysis from the manufacturer and country where the goods were manufactured must accompany all imports of food, drugs, cosmetics and items such as pesticides. All items entering the country must be labelled in metric terms.

All correspondence in respect of Product Registration should be addressed to thehttp://www.nafdacnigeria.org/ - http://www.nafdac.gov.ng

## Import controls

Inspection rules change frequently so exporters should check the requirements either with their customer, or with the relevant shipping company. The main inspection companies are:
http://www.sgs.com/
http://www.cotecna.com/COM/EN/Cotecna UK
http://www.intertek.com/
http://www.bureauveritas.com/

Although, Nigeria abides by World Trade Organisation regulations, clear communication with your local importer is vital to avoid misunderstandings and lengthy or costly delays.

All imports into Nigeria must be accompanied by a Manufacturer's Certificate confirming the standards used in production of goods.

Import licences are not required, but a system of destination inspection to verify the quantity and quality of goods imported is in operation. The Government of Nigeria has contracted with Cotecna for inspection services.

The Government of Nigeria has placed a ban on a variety of goods to protect local industries. It is illegal to supply customers in Nigeria via a third country, although goods from other West Africa countries are exempted if an Economic Community Of West African States (ECOWAS) form is presented to prove that they have been produced in that particular country.

A full list of prohibited imports can be obtained from the Nigerian Customs Service website or the Nigerian High Commission in London.

The Standards Organisation of Nigeria (SON) regulates the SON Conformity Assessment Program (SONCAP). Are the products that you are exporting covered by SONCAP? You can check this by visiting the SONCAP website.

## Import Restrictions

For details of prohibited goods visit the Nigerian Customs Service website or contact the Nigerian High Commission in the UK.

## Food, Drugs and Cosmetics

All foods, cosmetics and drugs that are produced or distributed in Nigeria must be registered with the National Agency for Food and Drug Administration and Control (NAFDAC).

## Value Added Tax (VAT)

VAT is a federal tax imposed on all goods and services, except those exempted and listed in the Schedule to the Act. For a list of exempted goods, please contact the Nigeria High Commission in the UK. VAT is a flat rate of 10%. The Federal Government doubled the rate of VAT from 5% to 10% with effect from 23 May 2007. In the case of imported goods, the value is taken to be the aggregate of cost, insurance and freight (CIF), plus custom duties and all expenses and other charges levied up to the port or place of importation. It is important that companies seek local advice on taxation as tax laws may vary between states.

## Double Taxation Agreement

Nigeria has a double taxation agreement with the UK. Thus, foreign tax paid may be credited against the total tax payable in Nigeria. Please contact HM Revenue & Customs for more information.

## Intellectual Property

Registration of Patents and trademarks is the responsibility of the Trademark Registry in Abuja. Registration gives exclusive use of the trademark or patent for seven years, which may then be renewed. Patents expire after twenty years.

## Exchange Controls

The government has already implemented most of the IMF's recommendations. Besides abolition of the two-tier exchange rate, the Central Bank of Nigeria (CBN) is now operating a market determined exchange rate policy.

## Terms of payment

Although all the common forms of arranging payment are in use in Nigeria, it is strongly recommended that exporters request payment in advance. This can be done either by cash or an irrevocable Letter of Credit confirmed by a reputable bank in Nigeria and reconfirmed by a bank in the United Kingdom.

## Getting your goods to the market

Lagos Port - Apapa and Tin Can Island - is the largest port in Nigeria with 20 berths and 15 warehouses. Port Harcourt, the second largest, has 9 berths. There are also ports at Warri, Sapele and Calabar. A free port operates at Onne, close to Port Harcourt, mainly servicing the oil and gas industry.

The Nigerian Ports Authority and the Nigerian Export Processing Zones Authority both have websites to provide further information on the export controls in Nigeria. Airfreight is mostly to Murtala Mohammed airport in Lagos, but also available to Kano in the North and Port Harcourt.

At present there is no air freight to Abuja. Freight forwarders should be approached as soon as possible rather than waiting until the goods are ready to send.

# Chapter 14: Methods of Conducting Business

AA Global Sourcing Ltd (http://www.aaglobalsourcing.com) can provide a list of lawyers and accountants if require.

All businesses in Nigeria must be registered with the Registrar-General of the Corporate Affairs Commission (CAC). Business activities may be undertaken as follows:
1. Private or public limited liability company;
2. Unlimited liability company
3. Company limited by guarantee
4. Foreign Company (branch or subsidiary company)
5. Partnership/Firm
6. Sole Proprietorship
7. Incorporated trustees
8. Representative office

## Registration

Registration forms are obtained from and submitted to the CAC, which requires the following additional documentation:
- Consent letters signed by a minimum of two directors
- Notice of the registered address
- Statement of authorised share capital of the company
- Memorandum and articles of association

The CAC will confirm receipt of the application, which usually takes two weeks.

**Representative Offices**

Foreign companies can set up representative offices in Nigeria. However, a representative office cannot engage in business, conclude contracts, open or negotiate any letters of credit.

It can only serve as a promotional and liaison office and its local operational expenses have to be paid by the foreign company.

A representative office must be registered with the CAC.

**The Export Credit Guarantee Department (ECGD)**

The ECGD is the UK export credit agency. It guarantees letters of credit to assist UK exporters to boost the availability of short-term export finance.

Please contact the ECGD directly for further information and terms and conditions at www.ecgd.gov.uk

# Chapter 15: Health & Safety

Nigeria has a number of health and safety laws. The Factories Act makes general provisions as to the standards of cleanliness, crowding, ventilation, lighting and drainage and the Workmen Compensation Act provides for the payment of compensation to workmen for injuries suffered in the course of their employment.

## Standards Organisation of Nigeria (SON)

The Nigerian Standards Organisation Act, 1971, established, as part of the Federal Ministry of Industries, the Standards Organisation of Nigeria (SON), to carry out the following functions:

- Designate, establish and approve standards in respect of meteorology, materials, commodities, structures and processes for the certification of products in commerce and industry throughout Nigeria;
- Provide necessary measures for quality control of raw materials and products in conformity with the standards specifications;
- Compile Nigerian standards specifications;
- Ensure compliance with designated standards
- Establish a quality assurance system including certification of factories and products

On the payment of a fee SON will provide the prescribed standards for a number of products.

## National Agency for Food and Drug Administration and Control (NAFDAC)

NAFDAC was established in 1993 to regulate and control the importation, exportation, manufacturing, advertisement, distribution, sale and use of food, drugs, cosmetics, medical devices, bottled water and chemicals.

No drug product, cosmetic or medical device can be manufactured, imported, exported, advertised, sold or distributed in Nigeria unless it has been registered in accordance with the 1993 Act.

# Chapter 16: Environmental Impact Regulation

The Federal Environmental Protection Agency (FEPA) is charged with overall responsibility for monitoring, supervising and co-ordinating necessary environmental impact assessments.

**Investing in Nigeria**

AA Global Sourcing Ltd (http://www.aaglobalsourcing.com) offers the following services to UK companies wishing to export to or set up a business in Nigeria.

There are a number of incentives to encourage both local and foreign investment in Nigeria.

Primarily EU funded, these incentives are aimed at upgrading the country's infrastructure.

Incentives are available to industry, but there is also a wide range of other EU incentives available to specific sectors such as construction, energy, commerce, agriculture, fishing and tourism. Conditions for application are governed by specific legislation for each incentive programme. The value of the incentive to be granted will be based on the technical evaluation of the project and on the Government's strategic plan.

Soil degradation; rapid deforestation; urban air and water pollution; desertification; oil pollution - water, air, and soil; has suffered serious damage from oil spills; loss of arable land; rapid urbanization

**Environment - international agreements**

Party to: Biodiversity, Climate Change, Climate Change-Kyoto Protocol, Desertification, Endangered Species, Hazardous Wastes, Law of the Sea, Marine Dumping, Marine Life Conservation, Ozone Layer Protection, Ship Pollution, Wetlands signed, but not ratified: none of the selected agreements

**Geography - note:**

The Niger enters the country in the northwest and flows southward through tropical rain forests and swamps to its delta in the Gulf of Guinea

# Chapter 17: Business Etiquette, Language and Culture

Many Nigerian businessmen and women are familiar with Western European business etiquette and culture. Many are young, well educated, and fluent in English, and have a very flexible business style.

Nigerian pidgin English, often known simply as 'pidgin' or 'broken' (broken English), is a widely spoken lingua franca, though with varying regional influences on dialect and slang.

## Hours of Business

The working week is Monday to Friday. However, in the largely Muslim Northern States, there may be some variation. The hours of work are normally between 0730 and 1730. Many companies favour an early start.

## Clothing

Most Nigerian businessmen wear a suit and tie or national costume at work. When visiting Nigeria, businessmen are advised to bring light weight suits or trousers and short-sleeved cotton shirts. Business women are advised to bring lightweight washable clothing. A lightweight raincoat and umbrella are useful during the rainy season.

Dry-cleaning facilities are only available in the major cities and are of variable quality. International hotels have laundry facilities at reasonable cost.

## Social Customs

In cities, cocktail parties and dinners are held, but generally less formal buffets are the norm.

Outside the predominantly Muslim areas women enjoy considerable freedom and play a large part in community and social life.

## Modes of address

Nigerians are very formal where titles are concerned and place a high degree of importance on them. Where relevant, titles such as Chief, Prince, Alhaja and Alhaji should always be used.

## Entertainment

There are a wide variety of restaurants in Lagos, but there is less choice in other cities. Restaurant meals cost between £10-20 per person. Nightlife in Lagos is very active and there are several nightclubs. Payment by credit card is not advised.

There are a number of cinemas and shopping malls in Lagos, such as The Palms, Mega Plaza, City Mall and Ceddi Plaza which cater to every shoppers need.

# Chapter 18: What are the Challenges?

## Security

Please visit the Overseas Security information for Business (OSIB) website for more information,

## Electricity

The mains electricity supply is unreliable, and generators are widely used in both home and work places

## Money

Nigeria is a cash economy. The local currency is the Naira, which exchanges for approximately 250 to £1. You should ensure that you bring enough currency (Pounds Sterling, US Dollars or Euros) to cover your costs. Travellers' cheques are difficult to cash in Nigeria. It is illegal to change money on the streets. Business people are strongly advised against the use of credit cards throughout Nigeria.

## Health

Basic medical facilities are available in some parts of Nigeria, while some states can boast of sophisticated facilities, though at a very high price. Malaria and polio are common to Nigeria and there are also regular outbreaks of cholera and measles. You should exercise normal precautions to avoid exposure to HIV/AIDS, which is more prevalent in Nigeria than in the UK.

Severe, but localised flooding has been known to occur in some parts of Nigeria during the rainy season. This can increase the threat of water-borne diseases. You should only drink or use boiled or bottled water. Avoid ice in drinks. If you suffer from diarrhoea during a visit to Nigeria, you should seek immediate medical attention.

You should seek medical advice before travelling to Nigeria and ensure that all appropriate vaccinations are up to date

**'419' fraud**

Advance fee fraud or '419' fraud (named after the relevant section of the Nigerian Criminal Code) is widespread. There are a myriad of schemes and scams via e-mail, faxes and telephone designed to facilitate victims parting with money. The vast majority involve requests to help move large sums of money with the promise of a substantial share of the cash in return.
Always refer such emails and fax messages to UKTI Nigeria.

**Contacts**

If you have a specific export enquiry about the Nigerian market which is not answered by the information on this book, you may contact:

UKTI Nigeria, Lagos
British Deputy High Commission
Commercial Section 11 Walter Carrington Crescent,
Victoria Island Lagos Nigeria.
Email: Commercial.Lagos@fco.gov.uk
Office Hours
0730 to 1530 Monday to Thursday
O730 TO 1230 Friday

Local time is one hour ahead of GMT and the same time as BST

# Chapter 19: Risks of Corruption

Petty corruption is reportedly widespread and surveys indicate that it is very hard to do business in Nigeria without having to pay facilitation payments to public officials.

State agencies tend to impose fees, licences, fines, and taxes arbitrarily. Some companies even report that they avoid posting signs identifying their factories, claiming that to do so would be an invitation to corrupt officials to stop by and solicit bribes!

Companies should note that property rights, contracts and commercial disputes can be difficult to enforce and settle in Nigerian courts due to corruption, inefficiency and under-staffing.

Tax administration lacks transparency which has led either to high levels of tax evasion or tax officials demanding bribes in return for lower tax rates. This practice is reportedly declining, but it still occurs.

Nigeria experiences heavy rainfall during the wet season (June - September) and flash flooding can occur. Water-borne disease poses a greater risk during the rainy season.

There is a high threat from terrorism in Nigeria. Attacks could be indiscriminate, including in places such as markets, hotels, shopping centres, places of worship and other areas frequented by expatriates and foreign travellers. Government and security institutions as well as international organisations have been attacked by Boko Haram.

There is a high risk of kidnappings and other armed attacks in the Niger Delta to ships and oil rigs at sea off the coast of the Delta. There is also a risk of kidnapping in other states in Nigeria. On 12 May 2011 a British citizen was kidnapped alongside an Italian in Kebbi State.

In recent months the Movement of the Emancipation of the Niger Delta has threatened to carry out attacks on oil and gas assets in the Niger Delta. The latest such threat was issued on 6 June 2011.

You should take out comprehensive travel and medical insurance before travelling.

# Chapter 20: Safety and Security

## Terrorism

There is a high risk of terrorism in Nigeria. You are advised to exercise caution and observe vigilance at all times, particularly in areas where there are political or other large public gatherings. Attacks could be indiscriminate, including government and security institutions, international organisations as well as public areas such as markets, hotels, shopping centres, places of worship and other areas frequented by expatriates and foreign travellers.

At approximately 10:20 local time on 26 August 2011 there was an explosion at the UN building in the diplomatic sector in Abuja. According to media reports, Boko Haram have claimed responsibility for the attack. Official sources have reported 23 casualties. Many more are reported injured. No British nationals are believed to have been caught up in the incident.

Recent attacks in Nigeria have - in the main - been carried out by two groups: Boko Haram and the Movement for the Emancipation of the Niger Delta (MEND).

Boko Haram is an Islamist extremist group. It has been responsible for an increased number of terrorist attacks across the north and attacked the National Police Force Headquarters in central Abuja on 16 June 2011.

MEND is a militant group seeking to assume control of Nigeria's energy resources in the Niger Delta region. A faction of MEND was responsible for the 1 October 2010 attack in Abuja. This attack demonstrated an ability and willingness of this faction to operate away from their usual base in the south. MEND has threatened to carry out renewed attacks on oil and gas assets in the Niger Delta

**Recent terrorist attacks include:**

On 26 August 2011 a car bomb exploded at the UN Headquarters in Abuja causing 23 fatalities.

There are regular attacks in public areas in Maiduguri, in Borno State, resulting in fatalities.

On 16 June 2011 a bomb exploded outside National Police Force Headquarters in central Abuja.

Over the 29 May 2011 presidential and gubernatorial inauguration, bombs were detonated in Bauchi, Zaria and Zuba, near Abuja.

There was a bomb explosion on 8 April 2011 at the offices of the Independent National Electoral Commission (INEC) in Suleja, Niger State, close to the capital city Abuja. This resulted in a number of fatalities.

Bombs exploded in Kaduna City, Kaduna State, on 7 and 16 April 2011.

Other serious attacks over the last few months have included:

On 31 December 2010, explosions at a restaurant in Abuja frequented by Westerners killed four people and injured nine others.

On 24 December 2010, a series of attacks in Jos in Plateau State killed around 80 people, including some attending Christmas Eve church services.

On 1 October 2010, three bombs exploded in central Abuja during Independence Day celebrations, killing twelve people.

# Chapter 21: Kidnapping

There is a high risk of kidnappings and other armed attacks in the Niger Delta targeting oil and gas facilities and workers. This also applies to ships and oil rigs at sea off the coast of the Niger Delta.

Since January 2007, we are aware of at least 24 British nationals and more than 200 foreign nationals who have been kidnapped in the Niger Delta area, with one British national being killed. Although there have been no reported kidnaps of Britons in the Niger Delta in the past year the risk remains and extends beyond the immediate Niger Delta area. Please see the local travel section for advice to help you ensure your own security while travelling in Nigeria.

There is also a risk of politically or financially motivated kidnapping throughout Nigeria. On 12 May 2011 a British citizen was kidnapped alongside an Italian in Kebbi State. A British citizen was kidnapped in Abuja on 22 June 2010, but was later released on 25 June. A non-British expatriate was kidnapped on 10 April 2011 in Abuja.

You should be aware that the long-standing policy of the British Government is not to make substantive concessions to hostage takers. The British Government considers that paying ransoms and releasing prisoners increases the risk of further hostage-taking.

# Chapter 22: Crime

Violent street crimes e.g. muggings, kidnappings, car-jackings and especially armed robberies continue at high levels in the south of the country. The prevailing situation even in comparatively safe areas of Lagos can change quickly, with periodic reports of street and car-related crimes. Most attacks happen after dark from 22:00 onwards. You should therefore limit road travel at night in Lagos as far as possible, especially away from the city centre - keep alert at all times.

British citizens should act upon any security advice given by their employers or, if visiting, their hosts. Avoid carrying large amounts of cash and wearing valuable watches, jewellery or items of sentimental value. Remain alert to your surroundings and the actions of local people around you. If you suspect danger, move away to a safer area. Do not try to resist.

There have been a number of robberies and kidnappings in Abia, Edo and Anambra States, in the latter particularly along the Enugu-Awka-Onitsha expressway. Travellers should exercise caution when driving outside cities, consider travelling in convoy, and avoid making any journeys that would involve travel after dark.

Experience has shown that, should you be unlucky enough to be caught up in an armed robbery, you should immediately comply with the attackers' demands. Those who have suffered injury or worse during such attacks have been perceived as not complying fully or quickly enough. The vast majority of those who endure such attacks, and follow this advice, do so without lasting physical harm.

# Chapter 23: Scams

Foreign nationals are frequently defrauded by scam artists. The scams come in many forms, and can pose great financial loss to victims. If you or your relatives or friends are asked to transfer money to Nigeria you should make absolutely sure that it is not part of a scam and that you have properly checked with the person receiving the money that they are requesting it.

Scam artists are also targeting individuals in the UK. There are a myriad of schemes in operation by West African criminal networks designed to facilitate victims parting with money, known as advance fee or 419 fraud.

Nigerian scam artists are also known to be targeting internet dating/personal sites with the intention of soliciting money from victims. For further information on advance fee fraud please see the West African advance fee Fraud Alert page on the website of the Metropolitan Police.

Foreigners, including Britons, are also targeted by scam artists they have met on internet chat rooms and on-line dating agencies. The scammer assumes the identity of an expatriate westerner and when trust has been established, sometimes over months or years, the victim of the scam is informed that their on-line friend in Nigeria is in trouble and in immediate need of funds. The reasons that the scam artists give for needing cash vary, but include being robbed or mugged, problems with airline tickets, being arrested at an airport for illegal immigration, being held against their will, being involved in a road accident (frequently on the airport road), hospitalisation, illness and advance payment for medical treatment. Many victims are persuaded to part with large amounts of money before they start to suspect anything.

If you are asked to transfer funds to Nigeria to help with a crisis you should ask the caller whether they have reported the incident (by phone or e-mail) to the British Deputy High Commission in Lagos.

We are also aware of a scam involving a fictitious "Basic Travel Allowance" fee requirement, which has become common. This is where it is alleged that the person trying to travel needs a certain amount of money before they will be allowed to travel. People have also received scam e-mails using commercial e-mail accounts (e.g. Yahoo, Hotmail, MSN etc.) allegedly from a British High Commission office in Nigeria requesting personal bank details, or for money to be transferred to High Commission staff. If you receive a report of a British national in Nigeria in distress or a request from any British High Commission office in Nigeria for bank details or money, you should immediately contact Consular Section, Lagos to investigate.

# Chapter 24: Powerhouses of Africa

Emerging markets from around the world are investing in the UK and all the while becoming important investment targets for UK businesses.

In the last decade, forward-thinking UK companies have fostered business opportunities in 'emerging markets' – those growing global economies which are expected to become international powerhouses over the next 40 years.

Commercial interest and activity from UK companies has highlighted the importance of rapidly expanding economies such as Nigeria.

By becoming significant developed markets in its own right, Nigeria will transform into vital trading partners, irrevocably changing the economic world-order.

Emerging markets such as Nigeria is "now viewed as sources of new consumer demand, ahead of simply being low-cost production hubs."

**Spotting potential**

UK companies have spotted the Nigerian potential and are investing in it accordingly. Business people simply want to know where the market is in their particular sector. So in the context of Africa, there has been a massive commodities boom.

This has solidified incomes and led to a growth of follow-on businesses, beginning in telecoms with mobile phone connections.

Nigeria has been identified as a growing consumer market. Yet alongside that, it now has a significant pool of people who have basic incomes, which has attracted big global consumer brands.

The Coca-Cola Company – one of the world's most visible brands with headquarters in Atlanta, USA, and bases across the UK – has recognised the importance of trading in emerging market like Nigeria.

A Coca-Cola Company spokesman said: "Over the next decade we anticipate that 70 per cent of the world's population will be in emerging markets, and the amount of money available to the consumers in these markets will double. By 2020, we believe the world will experience significant social and economic shifts, from a population increase of more than 800million people to nearly 900million moving into urban areas, and more than 1billion people joining the middle class.

"Populations are growing, economies are growing and the NARTD (Non-Alcoholic Ready to Drink) industry is relatively small. We work to be the first to gain access to a market and grow along with it by giving consumers access to our products and making them affordable. We often start with a very limited number of brands and package sizes and as the economy grows, so does our business."

## Global view

Louise Ingram is Director of Communications - Mobile Phones, at Nokia, the Finnish telecoms giant which has a Research Centre at the University of Cambridge. She highlights that Nokia has always thought it important to take a broad business view and tap into developing – as well as developed – economies.

Says Louise: "They say that necessity is the mother of invention. Nokia comes from Finland, a small country with a little over five million people. Nokia had no choice other than to 'go global' as the mobile communications revolution took hold in the early 1990s – and, throughout that decade, we secured strong footholds in key markets around the world including in Nigeria.

"Currently, while growth in the developed world is slowing, it is on the rise in many emerging markets. Because of our global reach and scale, Nokia is ideally placed to capture the growth and value ahead, especially in emerging markets. We are already on the ground with retail and distribution in all the BRIICA (Brazil, Russia, Indonesia, India, China, Africa) countries; we have local languages on our devices, we have local apps and we are already the market leader in Brazil, Russia, Indonesia, India, China and the majority of African and Middle Eastern markets."

## Strengthening presence

Similarly, leading UK companies have been operating in developing economies for some time. Manchester-headquartered consumer products company PZ Cussons, for example, operates worldwide, particularly in Nigeria; while London-based Inchcape, an international automotive distributor and retailer, operates in 26 mature and emerging markets.

Investment is also flowing the other way, with companies from emerging markets recognising the economic importance of doing business with UK companies. For example, there is valuable exposure to be gained by investing in leading British companies which do much of their business in Africa.

Yet emerging market companies have spotted huge direct investment opportunities too. As Business Secretary Vince Cable pointed out in a speech about emerging markets in September 2011, "companies from emerging markets like Tata and now the Thai steel company SSI are investing substantial amounts in the UK economy."

SSI, Thailand's largest steel producer, recently signed a memorandum of understanding with Corus to buy its Teesside Cast Products plant.

Win Viriyaprapaikit, President of SSI, said: "We have great respect for the tradition of steelmaking on Teesside and for the highly skilled Teesside workforce, having previously purchased slab from Teesside Cast Products." The transaction will enable

SSI to fulfil its long-standing objective of becoming a fully integrated steel producer with both melting and rolling facilities.

# Chapter 25: People

Population: 149,229,090

Country comparison to the world: 8

**note:** estimates for this country explicitly take into account the effects of excess mortality due to AIDS; this can result in lower life expectancy, higher infant mortality, higher death rates, lower population growth rates, and changes in the distribution of population by age and sex than would otherwise be expected (July 2009 est.)

## Age structure

0-14 years: 41.5% (male 31,624,050/female 30,242,637)
15-64 years: 55.5% (male 42,240,641/female 40,566,672)
65 years and over: 3.1% (male 2,211,840/female 2,343,250) (2009 est.)

## Median age

Total: 19 years
Male: 18.9 years
Female: 19.1 years (2009 est.)

## Population growth rate

1.999% (2009 est.)
Country comparison to the world: 59

## Birth rate

36.65 births/1,000 population (2009 est.)
Country comparison to the world: 30

## Death rate

16.56 deaths/1,000 population (July 2009 est.)
Country comparison to the world: 13

## Net migration rate

-0.1 migrant(s)/1,000 population (2009 est.)
Country comparison to the world: 92

## Urbanization

Urban population: 48% of total population (2008)
Rate of urbanization: 3.8% annual rate of change (2005-10 est.)

## Sex ratio

At birth: 1.06 male(s)/female
Under 15 years: 1.05 male(s)/female
15-64 years: 1.04 male(s)/female
65 years and over: 0.94 male(s)/female
Total population: 1.04 male(s)/female (2009 est.)

## Infant mortality rate

Total: 94.35 deaths/1,000 live births
Country comparison to the world: 13
Male: 100.38 deaths/1,000 live births

Female: 87.97 deaths/1,000 live births (2009 est.)

**Life expectancy at birth**

Total population: 46.94 years
Country comparison to the world: 212
Male: 46.16 years
Female: 47.76 years (2009 est.)

**Total fertility rate**

4.91 children born/woman (2009 est.)
Country comparison to the world: 32

**Major infectious diseases**

Degree of risk: very high
- Food or waterborne diseases: bacterial and protozoal diarrhea, hepatitis A and E, and typhoid fever
- Vectorborne disease: malaria and yellow fever
- Respiratory disease: meningococcal meningitis
- Aerosolized dust or soil contact disease: one of the most highly endemic areas for Lassa fever
- Water contact disease: leptospirosis and shistosomiasis
- Animal contact disease: rabies

Note: highly pathogenic H5N1 avian influenza has been identified in this country; it poses a negligible risk with extremely rare cases possible among US citizens who have close contact with birds (2009)

## Nationality

noun: Nigerian(s)
adjective: Nigerian

## Ethnic groups

Nigeria, Africa's most populous country, is composed of more than 250 ethnic groups; the following are the most populous and politically influential: Hausa and Fulani 29%, Yoruba 21%, Igbo (Ibo) 18%, Ijaw 10%, Kanuri 4%, Ibibio 3.5%, Tiv 2.5%

## Religions

Muslim 50%, Christian 40%, indigenous beliefs 10%

## Languages

English (official), Hausa, Yoruba, Igbo (Ibo), Fulani

## Literacy

Definition: age 15 and over can read and write
Total population: 68%
Male: 75.7%
Female: 60.6% (2003 est.)

## School life expectancy (primary to tertiary education)

Total: 8 years
Male: 9 years
Female: 7 years (2004)

## Education expenditures

0.9% of GDP (1991)
Country comparison to the world: 180

# Chapter 26: Communications

**Telephones - main lines in use**

1.308 million (2008)
Country comparison to the world: 69

**Telephones - mobile cellular**

62.988 million (2008)
Country comparison to the world: 16

**Telephone system**

General assessment: further expansion and modernization of the fixed-line telephone network is needed

Domestic: the addition of a second fixed-line provider in 2002 resulted in faster growth but subscribership remains only about 1 per 100 persons; mobile-cellular services growing rapidly, in part responding to the shortcomings of the fixed-line network; multiple cellular service providers operate nationally with subscribership reaching 45 per 100 persons in 2008

International: country code - 234; landing point for the SAT-3/WASC fiber-optic submarine cable that provides connectivity to Europe and Asia; satellite earth stations - 3 Intelsat (2 Atlantic Ocean and 1 Indian Ocean) (2008)

Radio broadcast stations:

AM 83, FM 36, shortwave 11 (2001)

**Television broadcast stations**

(the government controls 2 of the broadcasting stations and 15 repeater stations) (2001)

**Internet country code**

.ng

**Internet hosts**

1,098 (2009)
Country comparison to the world: 158

**Internet users**

11 million (2008)
Country comparison to the world: 29

# Chapter 27: Transportation Fact File

## Airports

56 (2009)
country comparison to the world: 83

## Airports - with paved runways

total: 38
over 3,047 m: 7
2,438 to 3,047 m: 12
1,524 to 2,437 m: 11
914 to 1,523 m: 5
under 914 m: 3 (2009)

## Airports - with unpaved runways

total: 18
1,524 to 2,437 m: 2
914 to 1,523 m: 13
under 914 m: 3 (2009)

## Heliports

3 (2009)

## Pipelines

Condensate 21 km; gas 2,560 km; liquid petroleum gas 97 km; oil 3,396 km; refined products 4,090 km (2008)

## Railways

Total: 3,505 km
Country comparison to the world: 49
narrow gauge: 3,505 km 1.067-m gauge (2008)

## Roadways

Total: 193,200 km
Country comparison to the world: 27
Paved: 28,980 km
Unpaved: 164,220 km (2004)

## Waterways

8,600 km (Niger and Benue rivers and smaller rivers and creeks) (2008)
Country comparison to the world: 15

## Merchant marine

Total: 68
Country comparison to the world: 62
By type: cargo 4, chemical tanker 12, Combination ore/oil 1, liquefied gas 2, Passenger/cargo 1, petroleum tanker 46, and Specialised tanker 2
Foreign-owned: 3 (Japan 1, South Africa 1, Spain 1)

Registered in other countries: 34 (Bahamas 2, Bermuda 11, Cook Islands 1, Georgia 1, Italy 1, Liberia 2, Panama 10, Poland 1, Seychelles 1, Sierra Leone 1, unknown 3) (2008)

## Ports and terminals

Bonny Inshore Terminal, Calabar, Lagos

## Transportation - note

The International Maritime Bureau reports the territorial and offshore waters in the Niger Delta and Gulf of Guinea as high risk for piracy and armed robbery against ships; numerous commercial vessels have been attacked and hijacked both at anchor and while underway; crews have been robbed and stores or cargoes stolen.

# Chapter 28: Nigeria Fact Files

Ease of doing business (rank) 125

Starting a business (rank) 108

Protecting investors (rank) 57

Procedures (number) 8

Extent of disclosure index (0-10) 5

Time (days) 31

Extent of director liability index (0-10) 7

Cost (% of income per capita) 76.7

Ease of shareholder suits index (0-10) 5

Minimum capital (% of income per capita) 0.0

Strength of investor protection index (0-10) 5.7

Dealing with Construction permits (rank) 162

Paying taxes (rank) 132

Procedures (number) 18

Payments (number per year) 35

Time (days) 350

Time (hours per year) 938

Cost (% of income per capita) 573.4

Profit tax (%) 21.8

Labour tax and contributions (%) 9.7

Employing workers (rank) 37

Other taxes (%) 0.7

Difficulty of hiring index (0-100) 0

Total tax rate (% of profit) 32.2

Rigidity of hours index (0-100) 0

Difficulty of redundancy index (0-100) 20

Trading across borders (rank) 146

Rigidity of employment index (0-100) 7

Documents to export (number) 10

Redundancy cost (weeks of salary) 50

Time to export (days) 25

Cost to export (US$ per container) 1,263

Registering property (rank) 178

Documents to import (number) 9

Procedures (number) 13

Time to import (days) 41

Time (days) 82

Cost to import (US$ per container) 1,440

Cost (% of property value) 20.9

Enforcing contracts (rank) 94

Getting credit (rank) 87

Procedures (number) 39

Strength of legal rights index (0-10) 8

Time (days) 457

Depth of credit information index (0-6) 0

Cost (% of claim) 32.0

Public registry coverage (% of adults) 0.0

Private bureau coverage (% of adults) 0.0

Closing a business (rank) 94

Recovery rate (cents on the dollar) 28.0

Time (years) 2.0
Cost (% of estate) 22

# Chapter 29: General Information

## Insurance

You should take out comprehensive travel and medical insurance, including a provision for medical evacuation, before travelling. You should check and exclusions, that you insurance company provides a personal insurance cover for you in Nigeria, and that your policy covers you for all the activities you want to undertake.

## Registration

British nationals staying in Nigeria for three months or more should register at the British High Commission in Abuja, the British Deputy High Commission in Lagos, our Liaison offices in Kaduna and Port Harcourt, or with the Honorary Consuls in Kano and Warri.

## Passports

As many crimes involve the theft of British passports, you should keep a photocopy of your passport, separately from the passport itself. This will speed up the process of issuing a new one.

## Consular Assistance Statistics

52 British nationals required consular assistance in Nigeria in the period 01 April 2010 - 31 March 2011

for the following types of incident: 15 deaths; two hospitalisations; and four arrests.

# Chapter 30: Conclusion

Nigeria have a business culture where negotiations are fluid and what's agreed on Monday might not necessary mean the same thing on Tuesday, how do you get the job done?

It's a challenge some foreigners encounter when doing business in Nigeria.

However, things don't have to be difficult, as long as you understand the cultural etiquette, doing business in Nigeria can offer vast opportunities. But, success comes down two key factors: contacts and commitment.

"The bottom line is that you cannot expect to go into Nigeria, make the deal, turn around, walk out and expect things to go as planned,"

You'll build friendships and relationships that will last a life.

If you're committed to business in Nigeria you have to know that you're entering an environment that requires your constant attention and constant renegotiation. Adaptability and flexibility on your part is key.

Knowing the right person is also fundamental, personal relationships are often more important than regulations and laws. It's something; many outsiders may feel uncomfortable with.

You have to be wary of the old tradition of 'dash,' which in Nigeria essentially means putting money in the hands of an individual.

It is of course in many respects illegal, but it is still quite a common convention and the degree to which you, as a business person, want to co-operate with this will determine to a great degree the success you have in Nigeria."

But despite the challenges, I am adamant business in Nigeria can be a rewarding experience and not just financially.

The people are fantastic; you realize that the social networks and relationships you put so some much energy and time into, are in fact is part of the great reward. You'll build friendships and relationships that will last a life.

**My top five tips for doing business in Nigeria**

1. Agreeing with people is considered to be a sign of respect. Nigerians generally say "yes" to a request because their respect for you does not allow them to say "no."

2. Among traditional Nigerian business people, an appointment is rarely private. Try not to be irritated if your meeting is interrupted by phone calls and/or visits from your client's friends and family.

3. Do not eat everything on your plate; leaving some food is a signal that you have had enough. If you

clean your plate, you are indicating that you want more food.

4. Nigerians tend to stand close to each other while speaking. If you are uncomfortable conversing at this distance, try to refrain from backing up.

5. Nigerians are good bargainers, and you should expect to bargain and compromise in the marketplace and at the negotiating table.

Good Luck!